"What a fun, inspiring, important and *true* story!
If one little dog can do so much for his community,
imagine what we all can do working together for our
own town, state, country and planet. Let's get to work!"

Sy Montgomery, author of the national bestseller The Good Good Pig
as well as 15 other celebrated nature books for children and adults

Bark! Bark! Bark for My Park!

by
Jessica Dimuzio, VMD
and
Johnny Angel

We all can make a difference!

Nature Tales and Trails, LLC
Norristown, Pennsylvania

Bark! Bark! Bark for My Park!

Copyright 2012 by Jessica Dimuzio All rights reserved.
ISBN: 978-0-9837839-0-9 LCCN: 2011933884
Website: www.naturetalesandtrails.com

Photographs by Timothy Wood with the exception of p. 3A & B, p. 9 background, p. 10 background, p. 13C, p. 20, p. 30, p. 31, p. 32A, and endpages by Tim Halverson; cover, p. 15, p. 21 and p. 32B by Jessica Dimuzio; p. 9 inset B by Joseph P. Gallagher.
Models: Mara Baker (as Jessica), Glover K. Campbell III, Christopher M. Carroll, Dennis R. Mellish, Michelle Brennan Ungaro, Josette Marie Ungaro, Amelia Grace Ungaro, Amy Brodsky, Alyssa Brodsky, Michael T. Wood, Ken Wise, Jeff Craig, Lily Magliente, Maia Magliente, Kirklynn Campbell, Roawoon Lee, Ruhri Lee
Canine Models: Johnny Angel, Holly Wood, Oreo Baker, Cutie Baker

Book design by Janice Phelps Williams

PRINTED IN THE UNITED STATES OF AMERICA

Cataloguing-in-Publication

Dimuzio, Jessica.

Bark! bark! bark for my park! / by Jessica Dimuzio and Johnny Angel.
-- Norristown, Pa. : Nature Tales and Trails, c2012.

   p. : ill. ; cm.

   ISBN: 978-0-9837839-0-9
   Audience: grades 2 and 3.
   Summary: "Told from the viewpoint of a five-pound Papillon puppy, [it] recounts the struggle of saving a 690-acre farm park from destruction. The story proves that no matter what size, age or species you are, you have the power to make a difference in your world if you use your voice, have passion and create a plan."--P. [4] of cover.
   Society of Children's Book Writers & Illustrators (SCBWI) Kimberly Colen Memorial Grant Award

   I. Norristown Farm Park (Pa.)--Juvenile literature. 2. Conservation of natural resources--Pennsylvania--Norristown Farm Park--Juvenile literature. 3. Environmental protection--Pennsylvania--Norristown Farm Park--Juvenile literature. 4. Civics--Juvenile literature. 5. Animal heros--Juvenile fiction. 6. Papillon dog--Juvenile fiction. 7. Dogs--Juvenile fiction. 8. [Norristown Farm Park (Pa.) 9. Conservation of natural resources. 10. Environmental protection--Pennsylvania--Norristown Farm Park. 11. Civics. 12. Animal heroes--Fiction. 13. Papillon dog--Fiction. 14. Dogs--Fiction.] I. Johnny Angel (Dog) II. Title.

PZ7.D598 B37 2012   2011933884
[E]   1201

ACKNOWLEDGMENTS

BARK! BARK! BARK FOR MY PARK! won the 2008 Society of Children's Book Writers & Illustrators Kimberly Colen Memorial Grant and the authors wish to thank the Colen family and the Grant Selection Committee for their recognition and support.

The authors greatly appreciate the encouragement and love from our family: Tim Halverson (husband, best friend, and pack leader), Jessica T. Dimuzio (mother extraordinaire), Marie Tofani (aunt and lover of R&B), and Bizou (joyous companion). We also acknowledge the support of our friends: the Baker family (Nita, Ken, Mara, Matt, Cutie Pie and Oreo), Donna Pratt and the Pratt Pack, Beth Preston, VMD, Bonnie Van Ormer, and Anne and John Pulliciano.

Without
  · casual comments by Elizabeth Kelly-Evans, Kimberly Glover, and Jo Ann Dalton;
  · excellent teaching and mentoring by Vivian Grey, Wendy Pfeffer, Pat Brisson, and Nancy Viau;
  · dogged support of the Milestones Children's Critique Circle, especially Jennifer Hubbard, Laurel Garver, and Kathye Fetsko-Petrie; and
  · enthusiastic encouragement from Mary Beth Lauer and Sy Montgomery,
this story would never have become a book. Thank you is not enough for the new and exciting adventures we are having.

Special acknowledgment and much appreciation is extended to Timothy Wood, nature photographer and Janice Phelps Williams, book designer, for their calm and steady manner in helping overcome the many hurdles on the way to creating a visually compelling book.

Telling the story with photographs would not have been possible without the co-operation and wonderful attitude of all my models, both human and canine. With much love and gratitude to Mara Baker who took the role of "Jessica" while the real Jessica directed the photo shoots and gave hand commands to the trained dogs.

Newspaper headlines and images are used with the permission of Stan B. Huskey, Editor, *The Times Herald*, with our thanks.

Thanks to the Montgomery County Department of Parks and Heritage Services and the Farm Park Preservation Association for working to keep the Norristown Farm Park safe and accessible as a working farm and passive recreation area in the middle of urban development.

A portion of the proceeds from the sale of this book will be donated to The Farm Park Preservation Association.

DEDICATION

We thank all those who work to save the natural environment, especially the Board and members of the Farm Park Preservation Association who are committed to preserve, protect, and promote the Norristown Farm Park.

We dedicate this book to the late Senator Edwin G. Holl whose vision preserved this land as a working farm park in the middle of urban development. The Norristown Farm Park is a place where city children can enjoy nature, see wildlife, and learn about farming.

BARK.
BARK.
BARK.
Let's go
to my park.

I bounce around the house with the leash in my mouth.

My owner Jessica ties her shoes and fluffs my fur. "Okay, Johnny Angel. *Let's go exploring.*"

Trotting to the Norristown Farm
Park, I stop to greet my dog friends.

A sniff here.
A sniff there.

What's new?

YIP. YAP. YIP.
It's my buddy,
Cutie.

She jumps *beside* me.

She jumps *behind* me.

She jumps right *on* me.

"Did you hear the *rumor*?" Cutie's owner asks Jessica. "People want to change this *park* into another golf course. We have dozens nearby. Everyone can use this park but not everyone can use a *golf course*."

Jessica shakes her head. "This is the only park in the state where city kids can enjoy nature and learn about farming." She glances down. "Johnny Angel, if they make a golf course, we'll lose our beautiful *woods* and *fields*."

My ears droop and my tail sags as we hike onto a forest *path.*

➡

Hurry. Scurry.

By the cornfield, a surprised groundhog flees between the stalks.

Whiff. Waft.

At the meadow, a musky fawn scent rises from warm grass.

Scritch. Scratch.

At the hollow oak, a sleepy raccoon

fixes his bed.

Splish. Splash.

At the stream, a great blue

heron fishes for his breakfast.

What will happen to these *animals* if they build a golf course here?

The next day, I fetch the newspaper. Jessica reads the headline:

Golf Plans for Farm Park

"Oh, no. The *rumor* is true. Johnny Angel, this park must be saved!"

Bark. Bark. Bark.
I agree. But what can a little puppy do?

I must do *something*.

I need a *plan*.

I *sniff* my food bowl, but I don't want to eat.

I *search* in my toy box, but I don't want to play.

I *circle* my bed, but I can't sleep.

I want a *plan*.

Looking out the door, I spy a squirrel on the bird feeder.

Uh oh.

I must *protect* the bird food.

Bark.
Bark.
Bark.

The squirrel stops, listens, and looks at me.

Bark!
Bark!
Bark!

The squirrel scampers away.

Hooray for me! My barking saved the bird food.

I wonder if *people* will listen to me?

Can I *bark, bark, bark* to save my park?

I dash to Jessica and pounce on the back of her leg. She looks down at my *wiggling* body.

I hop backwards. I wiggle harder.

"I know that *hop* and wiggle, Johnny Angel. You have an *idea*. Tell me."

Bark. Bark. Bark.

"I don't understand."

I scamper off. *Jessica* follows.

I grab the newspaper with the horrible headlines about the park and *shake* it hard.

"Drop it, Johnny Angel."

I drop the newspaper.

Bark. Bark. Bark. Bark! Bark! Bark!

"What a clever dog! You want us to bark, bark, bark for our *park*. We'll tell *everyone* we want to keep our farm park."

The next night, we attend a crowded town meeting.

Some people yell, *"Golf course."*

Others scream, *"Farm park."*

Voices rise louder and louder.

I stand on my chair. I puff out my chest. I raise my long *ears*.

Bark. Bark. Bark.
Bark! Bark! Bark!

People stop shouting.

They turn and they *stare*.

Jessica speaks to the crowd. "We need natural woods for hiking and wildlife. We need clean streams for fishing and grassy meadows for picnicking. We need farmland where kids can watch corn grow and feel fuzzy bean pods.

We *don't need* another golf course."

People *cheer*. But not everyone. Jessica and I must do more.

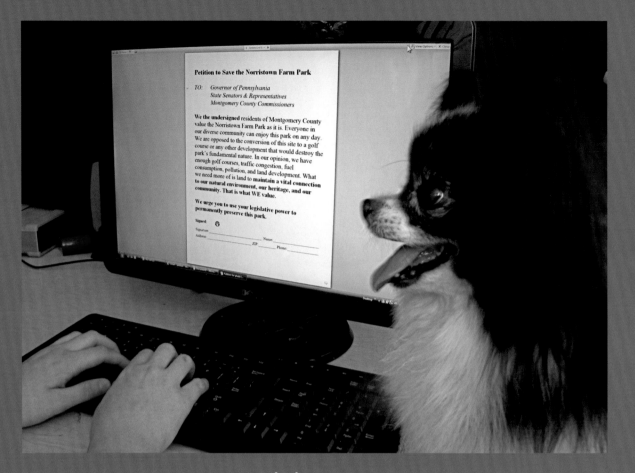

Jessica writes a *petition*. She reads it to me:

SAVE NORRISTOWN FARM PARK!

Protect wildlife.
Preserve woods and streams.
Keep corn and soybean fields.
PLEASE SIGN OUR PETITION, IF YOU AGREE.

Now each time we go out, I carry the petition in my backpack. We stop everybody we meet. Jessica asks them to sign the petition and I *bark, bark, bark* for my park.

Moms pushing strollers
write down their *names*.

Sweaty-browed joggers
stop to *sign* the paper.

Wading fishermen add their *signatures*.

In six weeks, we have **4,000** names.

Will that be enough?

Standing near the mailbox one day, I hear Cutie in the distance.

Yip. Yap. Yip.

Cutie runs down the street, pulling her owner.

"Look. We *won*!" Cutie's owner shows Jessica the headline.

"Johnny Angel, it's wonderful news. The park is *saved*!"

I jump with *joy*.
I wriggle with *glee*.

I roll over and *over*.

Cutie rolls over and over.

We *roll* over and over each other.

Jessica plops down on the grass.

"I wish we could thank all the people who helped save our park."

I rush over and lick Jessica on the cheek.

"Thank you for the puppy kiss, Johnny Angel. I wish you could kiss everybody who signed the petition.

Hmmm. Maybe you can.

Now I have an idea. Will you help me?"

I prance to the park. Jessica carries a big box with a sign:

KISSING BOOTH
I am Johnny Angel.
I want to kiss you for saving my park.

Jessica sets the box on
a picnic table, winks at
me, and I hop in.

Joggers and fishermen,
moms and their babies,
bird-watchers with
binoculars, all line up
to get *kisses*.

Bicyclists *cuddle* me.
The girls take off their helmets.
I kiss their cheeks.

Kids holding *lollipops*
rush up to me. I lick
an arm, an ear, a
nose.

Oops, a lollipop sticks
on my fur. I'll probably
get a bath tonight, but I
don't mind.

Now everywhere we go, people wave to me. I hear them tell their friends, "That little dog helped save our Norristown Farm Park."

Jessica crouches to hug me. "I'm so proud of you, *Johnny Angel*. You may be *little*, but your *voice* helped save this special place."

I hold my head high.

I wave my tail.

I'll always *bark, bark, bark* for *our* park!

ABOUT THE AUTHORS

Dr. Jessica Dimuzio graduated from the University of Pennsylvania School of Veterinary Medicine, specializing in wildlife preservation. She has conducted research on elephants, rhinos, and wild baboons and taught conservation programs in Africa, Asia, and North America. She has traveled to six continents to view wild animals in their natural habitats. In addition to writing about her adventures, Dr. D. loves to get kids excited about wildlife and the environment through her classroom talks and nature walks.

Johnny Angel, a graduate of Obedience I and II, Agility I, and a Good Citizenship Certificate Holder, reads to kids at the library, raises money for charity, and shares how he saved his park from destruction.

The authors live in Norristown, PA with Jessica's husband and Johnny Angel's girlfriend (a rescued Papillon). They hope you will join them in discovering the importance of animals in their natural habitats.

For more information about the authors, the park, school visits, guided nature walks, petition writing, educator resources, or additional book orders, please visit: www.naturetalesandtrails.com.

Johnny Angel was only two years old when he saved the park and the authors know you can **make a difference** too! Tell us how you have helped your school or neighborhood. Send us an email at: authors@naturetalesandtrails.com.

Dr. D.

"Bark! Bark! Bark for My Park! is a wonderful story for any age child. My students loved it..."
Mary Jo Seifert, Elementary School Teacher,
West Chester Area School District,
West Chester, Pennsylvania